Bingley
in old picture postcards

by
G. Firth B.A. Ph.D.

European Library - Zaltbommel/Netherlands MCMLXXXIV

GB   ISBN 90 288 2959 8 / CIP

European Library in Zaltbommel/Netherlands publishes among other things the following series:

IN OLD PICTURE POSTCARDS *is a series of books which sets out to show what a particular place looked like and what life was like in Victorian and Edwardian times. A book about virtually every town in the United Kingdom is to be published in this series. By the end of this year about 175 different volumes will have appeared. 1,250 books have already been published devoted to the Netherlands with the title* **In oude ansichten.** *In Germany, Austria and Switzerland 500, 60 and 15 books have been published as* **In alten Ansichten;** *in France by the name* **En cartes postales anciennes** *and in Belgium as* **En cartes postales anciennes** *and/or* **In oude prentkaarten** *150 respectively 400 volumes have been published.*

For further particulars about published or forthcoming books, apply to your bookseller or direct to the publisher.

This edition has been printed and bound by Grafisch Bedrijf De Steigerpoort in Zaltbommel/Netherlands.

INTRODUCTION

Bingley is a West Yorkshire town full of contradictions — a place where the old is jostled by the new. Farm lands run all the way up to factory walls and railway sidings; mullion windows can be found close by sash windows and the neo-Georgian portals of modern, semi-detached suburbia. Cobblestones run into asphalt and ancient quiet courtyards look onto thoroughfares busy with the bustle of modern living. For all its efforts to clamber onto the bandwaggon of modernity the town's old world atmosphere still occasionally peeps through with hints of the past, a well worn bridge over the river, the seclusion of its ancient parish church, the elegant antiquity of its town hall, but most of all, the sylvan beauties of Belbank Woods. Despite its industrial past the town has always had a reputation for rural tranquility, Victorians knew it as 'the Throstle Nest of Old England'.

Within the narrow gorge of Bingley, travellers can journey by road, rail and canal. The busy A650 passes over a mound of glacial moraine which forms the main street of the town; the main railway line to Carlisle and Scotland also runs through the town centre, parallel with the Leeds-Liverpool Canal. All three converge with the River Aire within a furlong's breadth to create a crowded Main Street.

In the earliest times Bingley was settled at the confluence of two secluded and well wooded valleys, and at a point where early man could quite easily ford the river and cross from one side of the valley to the other. By the seventh century there was a well established Anglo-Saxon community here, at the ley (meadow) of Binna's folk, as place-name evidence would suggest. This early settlement, with some Christian loyalty, was probably located on the present Bailey Hills site. The Romans seem not to have troubled Bingley although it is possible that the Roman road from Aldborough to Manchester passed through Cullingworth, Harden and East Morton.

In pre-Norman times Bingley was valued at £4 per year for tax purposes but like most West Yorkshire manors it is recorded in the Domesday Survey (1086) as 'waste' and assigned to an absentee manor lord. By 1140 the Augustinian monks of Drax Priory had been given much of the land in Bingley and were responsible for the building of a church, recolonising the town and creating new settlements like Priestthorpe. As more land came under cultivation the town had need of a market and this was granted by King John in 1212. With a town centre of church, bridge, corn-mill and market-cross the town eventually spread, ribbon-like, eastwards towards the end of the present Park Road.

Bingley seems to have weathered the storm of Scottish invasions and plague in the fourteenth century according to the Poll Tax returns of 1379, when the tax paid by Bingley far exceeded that paid by the inhabitants of Bradford or Leeds. This prosperity was probably based on the nascent woollen industry and is reflected in the rebuilding of the parish church and the founding of the grammar school by local yeomanry who also built fine homes for themselves at Gawthorpe, Harden, Greenhill and Marley.

Such men, seeking a more profitable income than that from farming, turned to the expanding wool textile industry producing a medium grade cloth which could be taken through all stages of production in a week and sold at the Cloth Halls of Leeds, Halifax and Wakefield.

During the eighteenth century an increased demand for cloth and improved technology created the need for specialised accommodation (as opposed to cottage production) and a strong source of power. Water powered spinning mills were established in the area after 1790 when Castlefields Mill was built. This industrial initiative of factory production occurred firstly along small remote tributary valleys like Harden Beck and Morton Beck. Bingley town's first textile factory (Providence Mill) was not introduced until 1802 when steam engines were available. There was, at this time, an increase in the town's commercial activity with the erection of the Market Hall (1753) in Main Street and with the building of the Leeds-Liverpool Canal (1770-1774).

A proliferation of textile factories in the town attracted a large work force and the township's population increased accordingly: Bingley 1801: 4,100; 1821: 6,176; 1841: 10,157; 1861: 13,254 and 1881: 18,437.

The houses built for Bingley's new population were either back to back or through terrace accommodation. Urbanisation of some scale occurred after 1847 on the town fields between the railway and the canal with streets radiating like spokes on a wheel from Seven Dials. The swelling of the town's population strained the traditional system of local government, the Vestry meeting of the parishioners. To meet the increased social problems like poverty, public health and crime control, an Improvement Commission was set up in 1847. A new burial ground was opened in 1870, sewage and water works were also begun by the Commissioners.

Voluntary elementary schooling at the National School (1814) was substantiated by the establishment of the Bingley School Board in 1875. The Mechanics Institute, opened in 1864, temporarily became the town's Technical Institute. In 1865 a public park was provided by public subscription. Chapel and pub competed for the communal life of the town but there were also numerous clubs and societies — sporting, political, musical, horticultural and dramatic.

But enough of this description of old Bingley. Let the written word stand aside for the fruits of the photographer's art.

1. 'Top o' Town' 1914. This area was one of the first to be transformed by intensive urbanisation provoked by the building of Peel Mill. To the right is Green's Yard which led by a series of alleyways and ginnels to Burrage Street. To the left are Ann Street (back to back terraces) and the Crown Hotel. Many of the buildings on the right were demolished in the road widening scheme of 1912.

2. Main Street 1900. Again at the junction with Chapel Lane (left) and leading up to 'Top o' Town'. The lamp post to the right leads to Myrtle Place. Also on the right is the King's Head Inn with its ample stabling for the old red & yellow coach.

3. Independent Chapel, Chapel Lane. Puritanism had early taken root in Bingley and the first dissenting congregation was that of Oliver Heywood's Independent Church, which was founded in Bingley in 1695 and they soon built themselves this chapel at the top end of Main Street. By the time this photograph was taken (1870) the Old Chapel was almost two centuries old and had been converted to meet Bingley's retailing needs, serving as a shirt making shop.

4. Quaker Hill. This building is the old Vine Tree Inn which was formerly the home of William Ellis, a corn miller and Quaker. Because of the association of Mr. Ellis the place came to be known as Quaker Hill or Quaker Steps.

5. Main Street. This wintry Main Street scene highlights two of the town's finest buildings. The Mechanics Institute (1864) and nearer the camera, the Co-operative Buildings which were built in 1887/88. The Bingley Industrial Co-operative Society was established in 1850 with an initial capital of £8 subscribed by eight working men. Its first premises were in a small cottage in Prospect Street but later moved to Chapel Lane.

6. Elm Tree Hill. A favourite site of Victorian Bingley but one that is difficult to visualise today. This hill was located opposite the end of Park Road on the Harden side of Main Street. The hill was crowned by an ancient elm tree which was in some state of decay even when the old hostelry was built in the late eighteenth century. A grand old sycamore took its place and here it was the custom for Bingley folk to gather round and discuss town affairs and politics. Much of the site was levelled off in the 1880's.

7. Elm Tree Inn about 1880. The tavern was well over a hundred years old when this photograph was taken. The inn served as a stage post for the Leeds-Skipton coach service which ran daily from 1817. A pack of hounds belonging to Mr. Birch of Myrtle Grove met here as did the huntsmen after the chase, to partake of the landlord's best beer. The inn, like all of Elm Tree Hill, was cleared away in the widening of Main Street in 1887.

8. Park Road End and Main Street about 1875. Park Road was formerly known as Toad Lane, a narrow but pleasant country lane. Here at the junction with Main Street is the old cottage of Harry Kendall, watchmaker. The larger buildings in the distance are Mechanics Institute (1864) and the Co-operative Buildings (1888).

OLD MARKET PLACE IN MAIN STREET, BINGLEY

9. Market Hall 1880. Here, on its original site in the middle of Main Street, since its erection in 1753 'at the considerable expense of £12.13.10½'. The building failed to revive Bingley's ancient agricultural market (1212) and when an outbreak of plague occurred in the town in 1787 many farmers took their produce to the Otley market and never returned. In 1888 the hall, cross and stocks were removed to the Prince of Wales Park to accommodate Bingley's urban development programme. The hall has recently been resited in the centre of the town.

10. Main Street about 1870. An unusual view looking up Main Street towards Park Road, from a position roughly opposite the Queen's Head Hotel. The centre of the picture is dominated by the Wesleyan Methodist Chapel (1790) built on land belonging to John Short, an early Methodist.

11. Wesleyan Chapel about 1875. This old chapel was built by the town's enthusiastic Methodist group in 1790. Here it serves the townspeople as an early shopping precinct. To the right is Robert Walker's tobacconist shop. The buildings were demolished in 1893.

12. The Strand, as this area was known in the lower part of Main Street. The houses to the left were built by the Vicar of Bingley, Dr. Hartley, in 1819. The premises to the right belonged to Mr. Wright, the saddler. These buildings were demolished in 1904 to make way for the new road.

13. New Main Street, Old Main Street. This important development scheme of 1904 created a new stretch of road which superseded the tortuous old highway which wound round the parish church. The new road meant disturbing the graves and memorials of old Bingley families. Work began on removing the 2,483 bodies in 1903 and a year later the new road was cut through. It meant the final demolition of the old Grammar School building and here Dr. Campbell Smith's cottage is about to disappear.

14. Old Main Street, 1900. An unusual view of the lower part of the town, from the Old Goods Yard behind the Hippodrome Cinema. To the rear of the Parish Church tower can be seen the new housing of Bailey Hills.

15. Old White Horse Inn, at the junction of Millgate and Old Main Street. There is reference to a hostelry here as early as 1379 although this building is thought to date from the seventeenth century. Like several other Bingley houses it carries the stone lanterns on either side of the gable to denote the former owners, Knights of St. John. Millgate to the left leads to Ireland Bridge and in the background on the other side of the river can be seen the premises of the Bingley Gasworks (first opened on this site in 1836) which had been purchased from a private owner in 1867 for £26,000.

16. Main Street 1890. With the clearance of the Wesleyan Chapel and old Market Hall the centre of Bingley was transformed. On the south side some fine new buildings appeared like the Midland Hotel (1892) far left. This open, tree-lined boulevard is a considerable civic improvement on the dingy 'olde worlde' arrangement of the earlier period.

MAIN ST BINGLEY.

17. Lower Main Street about 1895. An interesting view of the Main Street before the new road was cut through the cemetery in 1904. On the extreme right of the picture are the premises of George Slicer, producer of mineral waters and mine host of the Queen's Head. The old cottage in the centre is home and smithy of Robert Longbottom whose family occupied the premises as blacksmiths for nearly three hundred years. The building was originally a farm house. Here the house stands above street level but before the road improvements of the 1870's, it was necessary to descend two steps from the street into the premises. The smithy was demolished in 1912 to make way for the Hippodrome Cinema.

18. 'The Balconies'. Working class housing built in the 1890's on the former Elm Tree Hill site, they stretched all the way to the riverside by means of this ingenious tiered system. They resembled modern flats of which one visitor wrote in 1906, 'the only entrance I could find either back or front being by means of a balcony, the other end of which was on a level with the street high above. Damp linen was floating in the breeze and children were playing about. Just the sort of place children revel in. Romantic to a degree!' The railings to the left skirted the old corn mill weir.

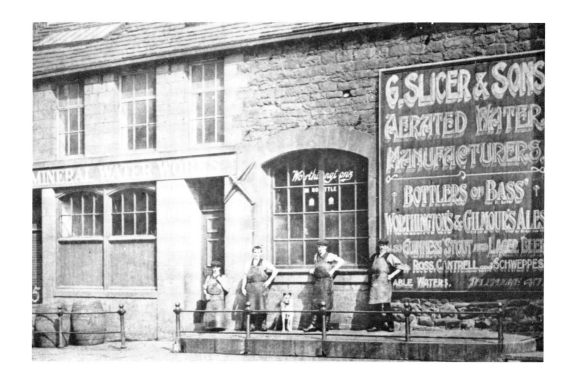

19. Slicer's yard was on this site though formerly known as Mary Jowett's Yard. She was landlady of the Old Queen's Head and was succeeded in that position by George Slicer who also owned the mineral water works nearby. Here lived the 'old town crier' Mr. Crowther.

20. Keighley Road after the new road had been put through the cemetery in 1904 when, it is said, the navvies made small fortunes at the pawnbrokers on rings taken from the disturbed graves. To the left are the premises of the Strand stores and café on the site originally known as the Strand. Lower down on the same side is the Fleece Hotel. Note the tram lines set in the cobbles of Main Street. It was at this time that the present Old Main Street became somewhat redundant.

21. Bellman Row, about 1910. This short street linked the new Keighley Road to the Old Main Street. The wall to the left is the boundary of the churchyard.

PARISH CHURCH FRONT VIEW

22. Parish Church. This postcard shows the inside and exterior of the ancient Parish church. The greater part of it, is sixteenth century with the choir built in 1518 by Reverend Richard Wylson. The top story of the tower and its battlements was added in 1739. Inside, the Perpendicular style is apparent in the lower chancel where there are five bays with octagonal piers.

23. Parish church and Graveyard. A view of the church tower and nave from the old graveyard which was obliterated by the new Keighley Road. Many of the interesting old gravestones were lost or removed during the road construction, including that of John Nicholson, poet of Airedale. When the old churchyard became full and unhealthy there was considerable local debate as to where a new burial ground should be located. Finally in 1869 the Burial Board chose Bailey Hills and the new cemetery was opened in 1871.

24. Storm over Bingley. An electric storm lights up the town in this striking photograph. The spire of Mornington Road Wesleyan Chapel (1874) looks vulnerable surrounded by all the fork lightning.

25. Main Street about 1930. You can almost hear the hubbub of a busy city — what a change from the rural market town of late Victorian times. The straightening of Main Street (by the church) enhanced the introduction (1914) of electrically powered trams but here Bingley is very much in the motor car age.

26. View across Bingley 1910. A view of the west side of the town from Altar Road. In the foreground is the cluster of houses in Old Main Street. The photograph is dominated by the massive Bowling Green Mills (now Damart) built in 1871 by S. Wildman & Son to spin worsted yarn on 25,000 spindles. To the left of the picture Albert Mills, built two years earlier (1869) by Platts & Co.

27. Park Road. Shopping on horseback in Park Road between the wars. Much of the housing in this area went up in the period 1880-1914 and provided homes for the artisans and lower middle classes of Bingley. Top right is the woodland and estate of John Barron's 'Claremont'. Barron was a successful coal merchant, JP and chairman of Bingley council.

28. Leach and Jennings. An old Main Street residence (1706) located shortly before the entrance to Elm Tree Hill. Like everything else in Main Street it changed in the 1880's and became a hosiery shop run by Mrs. Jennings and her daughters. To the left are the premises of her husband, a local butcher.

A much earlier view of the same building before the street level was changed and showing the original location of the date stone. This building situated opposite the Mechanics Instiue came to be well known this century as the hardware premises of Hebden & Holding (demolished 1974).

29. Hebden & Holding. The same building in the twentieth century with its familiar wood and plaster façade. The site was cleared in 1974 to make way for the new Bingley Arts Centre.

30. More Main Street shopping premises showing the tailor's shop of George Whitaker. At front, the waifs and strays of Victorian Bingley gather 'en masse' to have their 'picture took' displaying a wide variety of headgear.

31. King's Court about 1890. This shows the ancient court with its seventeenth century housing. The carriage entrance leads to the cobbled courtyard of the Ferrands Arms, one of Bingley's nineteenth century hostelries. To the left are Queen Street and Liverpool House which later became the post office (1893).

32. Post office about 1900. The first post office was located at Joseph Richardson's house in Main Street but moved here in 1893, at the junction of Main Street and Queen Street. These premises were soon inadequate and a new post office was opened on the old Market Hall site in 1914.

33. Bingley postmen about 1914. In 1877 there were just two postmen to do the twice daily deliveries around the town, Beckfoot and Gilstead. There were only three pillar boxes in Bingley, at Park Road, York Place and the top of Ferncliffe. The first sub-post office was opened at Gilstead in December 1892. Here James Allen (far left) poses with his 17 colleagues outside the Queen Street office. Allen retired in 1919 after 42 years service in the Bingley post office.

34. Myrtle Place about 1914. To the left are the premises of the ancient Bingley Court of Requests (1831) which was a small court for defaulting debtors. Further along, the building with the heavy cornice and arched windows was the old Police Court House (1860) which occupied the site of the old lock-up and workhouse.

35. Main Street about 1935. Right, can be seen the setts of Park Road. At centre is the service tram to Crossflatts. In addition, the town was linked to neighbouring towns by the Premier bus company, and later the West Yorkshire company. Here the Bradford-Crossflatts service is about to pull out in the direction of Saltaire.

36. Seven Dials about 1890. The streets of the Bingley working class quarter radiated off this favourite meeting point like spokes on a wheel. The street-ends in view here are, from left to right, Hill Street, Church Street, York Street. The photographer is standing at the junction of Chapel Lane and Wellington Street. The building, centre right, is the old Malthouse.

37. Eldon Place. These houses are typical of the accomodation that went up to house Bingley's growing working classes (mostly textile workers) in the nineteenth century. This small quadrangle was to be found between Ebor and Victoria Mills with the Canal to the north west. The houses to the right are the backyards of North Street.

38. Ferncliffe about 1900. An outpost of Bingley for much of the nineteenth century, Ferncliffe came into its own with the enclosure of Gilstead Moor in 1861, and the construction of working class housing at Dubb Mill in 1888. Ferncliffe was chosen by Bingley U.D.C. as a large estate for its council house programme in the 1930's.

39. Raven Royd Farm. One of the most ancient of farms in the outlying area, possibly dating back to
Viking times. It was certainly referred to in the Poll Tax of 1379. By the late-seventeenth century
Ravenroyd was a known centre of the Quaker faith in the shape of the Maud family. Situated at a
bend in the River Aire it had become a favourite walk for Bingley folk in the late-nineteenth century
and like so many other local farmhouses, was famed for its farmhouse teas!

40. Beckfoot Farm about 1870. This fine old farmhouse was erected in 1617 by the Rawson family. This is another site formerly owned by the 'soldier priests' — the Knights of St. John. The farm in this photograph is still very much a working farm although at one time the centre of a busy trade in woollen cloth.

41. Milner Field. This magnificent pile was built in 1874 by Sir Titus Salt for his son of the same name. Equipped with all the modern conveniences this beautiful residence was built upon a commanding eminence with panoramic views over the Aire Valley. King Edward VII and his queen stayed here as Prince and Princess of Wales when opening Bradford Technical College in 1882. Five years later, May 1887, Princess Beatrice and Prince Henry of Battenburg stayed at this house before the opening ceremony of the Saltaire Jubilee Exhibition. The fortunes of the house were closely linked to those of the Salts mill and consequently it fell into disrepair and neglect after 1914.

42. Here, on a rainy day, Chairman of the Bingley Urban District Council, Sam Rushforth, welcomes General Booth, founder of the Salvation Army, to the town. The Bingley church met in its 'barracks' in Russell Street.

43. Shortly before the First World War there were three bowling clubs in existence at Park Road, Cottingley (1903) and here at what is thought to be Slenningford, where the opening match is taking place on 27th May 1901.

44. Market Hall. This 'shed' served Victorian Bingley as a covered market until it was knocked down in 1913 to make way for the new post office. The shop on the left of the picture was occupied by Mr. J. Pratt, men's outfitters. The shed was located below the Midland Hotel and across the Main Street from the Queen's Head Hotel.

45. Bingley Fair 1904. By 1850 Bingley had become an industrial town rather than a farming centre. However its market continued to be held each Tuesday. Its two annual fairs (one in January for horned cattle, the other in late August for horses and merchandise) also survived into the twentieth century. Here, in 1904 are stalls for sale of coconuts, brandy snap and drinks at Bingley 'tide' or 'feast' as it became known. The Gas Field was used as a fair ground. In the corner nearest the gasworks' gates there was invariably a show. Here, the first cine-pictures were shown in Bingley. Dancing girls in front of the booths attracted the crowds.

46. Gooseberry Championships, 1912. The opening of the Cottingley allotments in 1844 proved particularly successful for the growing of gooseberries. This led to gooseberry shows which in 1877 were open to all England. The national championships were held in Bingley until the outbreak of war in 1914. Many were held in public houses for example Star Inn, York Street. Here, in 1912, Oliver Mitchell from Morton is the chief official at the weigh-in which was conducted with all the solemnity of a religious rite.

47. Bingley Show, about 1950. In 1862 a ploughing society was formed in Bingley and the first contest was held that year. The three classes attracted 37 competitors. This was followed by a dinner at the Old Queen's Head provided by landlord George Slicer. Competitors committee and judges all attended. Shortly afterwards the Bingley Agricultural Show was founded and held in a field at Gawthorpe. In 1869 it moved to Myrtle Pasture where it was held until 1908 when that site was claimed for a massive housing project. It then was transferred to the Grammar School Field.

48. Morecambe or Bingley-on-Sea. The Bingley show was an important feature of the 'Bingley Tide' or 'feast'. For those with a greater sense of adventure and a little more money, there was the trip to the seaside at Blackpool or Morecambe. Bingley folk tended to favour Morecambe.

49. South African war memorial ceremony. British imperialism in all its military splendour came to the town in June 1905 when memorials at the Parish Church and Town Hall were unveiled in honour of Bingley men who had served in the Boer War. Bands paraded up and down Main Street throughout the day as high ranking officers presented medals to the forty odd men who had served and unveiled a plaque in the Parish Church to the three men who had died on active service. Here the procession is just passing the end of Park Road with the Midland Hotel to the left.

50. Seven Dials 1897. To celebrate Queen Victoria's Diamond Jubilee in 1897 the council raised these celebratory wooden arches at strategic points about the town, all illuminated by gas of course. Beneath these triumphant arches at the end of Church Street there passed a massive procession of historical tableaux depicting Bingley's history. To the left is Mr. Kershaw's shop.

51. Bingley Rugby Club 1893. A fine athletic body of men from the Bingley Rugby Football Club which was established in 1876. This team won the Yorkshire No. 3 Competition Shield by defeating Hebden Bridge 7-3 in a play-off at Manningham before a crowd of 6,000. Skipper (seated with shield) was Tom Broadley who went on to represent England on six occasions and gain 38 caps for his county.

52. Flood damage at Morton 1900. On 12th July 1900 a terrific storm broke on Rombalds Moor. The still warm summer weather suddenly gave way to a downpour of heavy rain which lasted for three hours. Water poured off the moor into one major current, Morton Beck at Sunnydale. This was quickly transformed into a Niagara. Roads were swept away as inhabitants took themselves and their belongings upstairs. There was no loss of life but several cottages and all the mills were damaged. That evening marooned women and children were rescued from bedroom windows.

53. Bingley National School about 1870. One of the earliest surviving National Schools in the country, built before the days of Waterloo (in 1814)! After a precarious early existence the school benefitted from the 1833 Factory Act which compelled children in the surrounding textile mills to receive two hours education each day. An interesting photograph notable for the typical Victorian gentleman in the foreground and for the little chap on the right who is obviously where he shouldn't be. To the left can be seen the debris following the boiler explosion of 1869.

54. Bingley boiler explosion 1869. This was the scene following Bingley's worst disaster on 9th June 1869 when a faulty mill boiler belonging to Messrs. Town & Sons exploded, killing fifteen people. Most of them were children of the Bingley National School in Lime Street whose playground adjoined the mill. The school became a mortuary as frantic parents clawed with their bare hands through the masonry and ironwork to reach the pitiful cries of young children trapped beneath the rubble. There was a great cheer ten hours after the explosion as rescue workers removed an over-turned skep to find one child — fast asleep! These postcards and others were sold to raise money for the disaster fund.

55. Bingley Grammar School, 1912. Here, Mr. Walter Dazeley, headmaster, is seated with all the boys of the Grammar School in front of the old school building first erected on the Auction Mart site in 1856. Dazeley was head from 1902 to 1918 and piloted the school through a period of massive change.

56. Bingley Grammar School about 1906. Boys of the Grammar School seated at their desks in one of the new classrooms, part of the new building opened in 1906 by A.H.D. Acland, Minister of Education. The parents of these boys paid fees which were fixed between £3-8 except for two fortunate young men who were awarded foundation scholarships each year.

57. Bingley Mechanics Institute, currently unused and in a state of disrepair. This building has served Bingley folk well in its short life. It was built in 1864 on the site of an old iron foundry, by working men who had formerly met in rooms in Russell Street. In its early days the Institute was attended by over 350 members who made use of a fine library of 6,000 volumes. During the 1880's the committee began classes in both arts and science, both of which were taken over by the Technical School in 1889. Since then the building has served as Girls' Grammar School, public library and town hall. Its future is in doubt.

58. Myrtle Park School, 1908. Opened its doors to the children of Bingley in 1907. Situated in an expanding neighbourhood it replaced the old Hill Street Methodist School. It provided accommodation for both mixed and infant departments. There were three entrances for girls, boys and infants. This was the first school erected in Bingley under West Riding Management following the 1902 Education Act.

59. West Riding College 1911. This college for the training of women teachers was officially opened in October 1911. Here it is in an advanced stage of construction. The college was built on the Lady House estate which belonged to the trustees of the Grammar School for many years.

60. Bingley teacher training college. Here are some of the earliest students, in residence in Ascham Hall. The lady (front right) is Dr. Helen Wodehouse who was appointed principal of the college in May 1911, when the college opened. The college provided 200 places for young women from all kinds of social backgrounds. On the left is Miss Davis. Below another group of students in residence at Hild Hall in 1912.

61. Ireland Bridge. An unusual view of the town taken from the river just beyond the weir. The tower in the centre belongs to the old fire station. The chimney and mill are on the site of the mediaeval corn mill. The river had always been crossed at the bottom of Belbank wood or by the stepping stones at the bottom of Ferrand Lane. Throughout the middle ages the wooden bridge was used by pedestrians and horses but not carts and by 1683 it was in a serious state of disrepair. A wider stone bridge was built in 1686-87.

62. Cottingley Bridge about 1900. This bridge carries the main Bradford-Keighley road and provides the main entrance to Bingley town on what was formerly Leeds Lane. Until 1683, when it was rebuilt of stone, travellers had journied down the narrow and remote highway of Beckfoot Lane, entering the town via Ireland Bridge and Millgate.

63. Toll bar at Cottingley. This vestige of the old turnpike trust system was finally demolished in 1913 when Cottingley Bridge was widened to accommodate the construction of an electric tramway and the growth of motor traffic.

64. Leeds-Liverpool Canal. This is the rather elegant steam craft 'Water Witch' used by the directors and special customers of the Leeds-Liverpool Canal Company just before the First World War. Top left, behind the trees, are Bingley's ancient Elizabethan homestead, Gawthorpe Hall and its Falconry. The boat has just reached the top of Five Rise Locks and is heading west towards Skipton.

65. Five Rise Locks 1928. This steam-driven short boat prepares to leave the staircase of five locks, loaded with coal. The locks were opened in 1774 amid great local rejoicing and celebration. The first barge took 28 minutes to descend the locks. At the summit, can be seen the lockkeeper's cottage.

BINGLEY—THE CANAL AND THREE RISE LOCK.

66. Three Rise Locks. Joe Salt, a well known local boatman, gets ready to take the Skipton Co-operative Society boat through the locks as the horse is led up the tow path past the lock-keeper's cottage (top left). To the right are the massive premises of the Bowling Green Mill (1863).

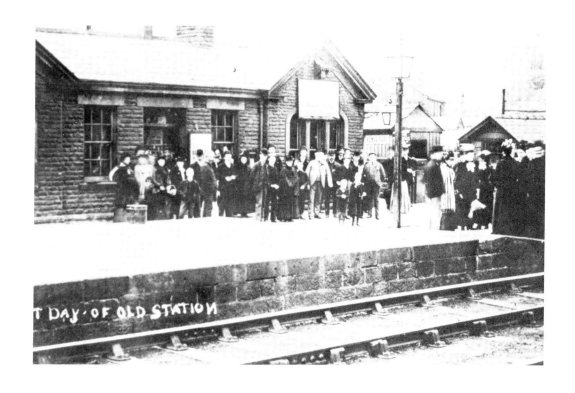

67. Old railway station 1892. Here at the closing ceremony the dignitaries were relieved to see the end of this old fashioned station, close to the goods yard; Three-Rise Locks and Bowling Green Mill. There had been repeated level-crossing accidents.

68. Railway station, 1892. Bingley was first placed on the railway map in 1846-47. The first station was situated in Dean's Yard (near present station on Park Road corner). The second resiting took place in July 1892 when the station moved from the goods yard site to this location in Wellington Street.

69. Bingley's First Electric Tram. The electric tramway was first brought to Bingley in 1914 as part of the Bradford system. It went only as far as Crossflatts. Here Labour County Councillor Tom Snowden (Lab) addresses the crowd on the opening of the tramway in Bingley.

70. Hippodrome Cinema, 1952. This was built on the site of the old smithy in 1913. It had a seating capacity of 750 and was the first of the town's cinemas to introduce 'talkies'. The Hippodrome and Herbert Upton were synonymous. Upton served the picture palace as electrician, film operator and manager in his 40 years service. In 1953 the cinema became a large department store, Woolworths. It has recently been demolished.

71. Myrtle Cinema. At one time Bingley had four cinemas: Gem Picture House, Hippodrome, Co-op Hall and this one, the most recent and perhaps best remembered. It was built in 1921 on the site of the ancient Hoyle Croft, a grass covered square overlooked by the backs of houses in Chapel Lane and Main Street.

72. Oddfellows Hall, 1968. Many Bingley folk will best remember this building as the old Bingley Little Theatre, but it was erected in Waddington Street in 1862 as the Oddfellows Hall. The Oddfellows were a friendly society who had met in a cottage adjoining the Ferrand's Arms until they could afford to build these premises. By 1895 they had 1,600 members and held an annual procession and church service. The Hall became a public hall for many social and political occasions. The photograph shows the main entrance to the Little Theatre.

73. Old Brown Cow Inn. Sited on the Harden side of Ireland Bridge, this old tavern served as a meeting place for the trustees of the Keighley-Bradford Turnpike Trust. Here too the Petty sessions were held until the local magistrate moved to more functional premises and left the room to a former grammar school master who ran a small independent school. This building is best known for its associations with the climax of the Chartist riots in 1848 when 16 local men were arrested by Squire Ferrand. The premises were stormed by a mob of working men who released the prisoners and attacked the magistrate.

74. Dick Hudson's 1914, as it is familiarly known (more correctly The Fleece). It was formerly the site of Highgate Farm whose owner Tommy Anderson acquired a liquor licence. In 1809 the farm and pub were bought by Thomas Hudson whose son Dick kept the inn from 1850 to 1878. This present building was put up in 1904. Dick Hudson's was a favourite holiday spot for thousands of working people who tramped the moors around it, secure in the knowledge that they would be well served with its traditional fare of roast beef and Yorkshire pudding (1/- per head) or the famous 'am n' egg tea. At the time of this photograph James Clarke was mine host.

75. Mobilisation 1914. Members of the Bingley Volunteer Training Corps march past Albert Fortune's shop at Poplar House. The recruitment office was at the Town Hall (Mechanics Institute) where Dr. Angus and Dr. Crocker gave the men medical examinations. Here the young men of Bingley march out of the tranquility of the 'Throstle Nest of Old England', and into the holocaust of twentieth century warfare.